UNIVERSITY *of* CAMBRIDGE
ESOL Examinations

WITHDRAWN

Top Tips for IELTS
Academic

Produced by Cambridge ESOL
in collaboration with the British Council

Acknowledgements

Cambridge ESOL would like to thank the following for their contributions to this project:

Margaret Matthews, Felicity O'Dell, Michael Black and Carole Allsop.

Every effort has been made to identify the copyright owners for material used, but it has not always been possible to identify the source or contact the copyright holders. In such cases, Cambridge ESOL would welcome information from the copyright owners.

Illustrations by Sandra Lockwood, Artworks Design.

University of Cambridge ESOL Examinations
1 Hills Road, Cambridge, CB1 2EU, UK
www.CambridgeESOL.org

© UCLES 2009

First published 2009
Printed in the United Kingdom by Océ (UK) Ltd

ISBN: 978-1-906438-72-2

Contents

KT-441-401

Introduction

Top Tips for IELTS is an essential part of your revision for the International English Language Testing System (IELTS) test.

Each of the four main sections (Listening, Reading, Writing and Speaking) follows the same structure and is based on a series of pieces of advice (the 'tips') which IELTS' materials writers have collected from many years' experience of involvement in the production of IELTS tests. Each section starts with a tip at the top of the page. The tip is followed by an example taken from IELTS material and a clear explanation to help you understand exactly what it means. Each section ends with some more 'General tips' for that component.

There is also a handy section at the beginning of the book on how to revise for IELTS and a very important section at the back on what you should do on the day of the test.

There is a companion publication to this book, *Top Tips for IELTS General Training*. Please note that the Listening and Speaking sections are common to both books.

IELTS is jointly managed by British Council, University of Cambridge ESOL Examinations (Cambridge ESOL) and IDP: IELTS Australia.

How to use *Top Tips for IELTS*

Take the *Top Tips for IELTS* book with you and read it when you have a few minutes during the day. Then use the CD-ROM to practise at home: it contains an IELTS practice test for you to try, together with the answers for Listening and Reading and some sample answers for the Writing. The CD-ROM also includes all the recordings for the Listening and a video of a candidate doing an example IELTS Speaking test, to show you exactly what you will have to do when you take the test. Practise with some classmates using the Speaking test material on the CD-ROM and compare your performance with the student on the video.

Top Tips for IELTS is flexible. You can look at a different tip from a different section every day, or you can start at the beginning with the tips for the Listening test and work through until you get to the end of the tips for the Speaking test. Whichever method you prefer, read the example and the explanation carefully to make sure that you understand each tip. When you have understood all the tips for each section, try the test on the CD-ROM.

Guide to symbols

This symbol introduces the 'tip' which is at the top of the page. Each tip is some useful advice to help you find the right answer for Listening and Reading. For Writing, the tips show you how to write a better answer to the question, and for Speaking, they explain how you can give good answers which show your true level of English to the examiner.

This is an extra piece of advice which is important for this particular part of the test.

This symbol tells you to go to the CD-ROM, where you will find an IELTS practice test to try.

We hope that *Top Tips for IELTS* will help you with your preparation for taking the IELTS test.

Cambridge ESOL

Guide to question types used in IELTS Reading and Listening

Multiple choice *(Listening and Reading)* You have to read a text or listen to a recording and answer some questions. In Listening multiple-choice tasks, you usually have to choose one of three possible answers (A, B or C) for each question; in Reading you usually choose one of four (A, B, C or D). In some multiple-choice tasks, you have to choose several options from a longer list.

Identifying information *(Reading)* You have to read a text and a series of statements and decide if the statement agrees with the information in the text ('true'), if the statement contradicts the information in the text ('false') or whether there is no information in the text to support the statement ('not given').

Identifying writer's views/claims *(Reading)* You read a text and a series of statements and say whether each statement agrees with the views/claims of the writer. For each statement, you answer 'yes' if the statement does, 'no' if the statement doesn't, or 'not given' if there is no view/claim in the text to support the statement.

Matching information *(Reading)* You have to locate specific information in a paragraph or section of a text.

Matching headings *(Reading)* You have to choose the correct headings for the paragraphs or sections of the text.

Matching features *(Reading)* You have to match numbered items to a set of features (e.g. people or dates) from the text.

Matching sentence endings *(Reading)* You are given the first half of a sentence based on a text and you choose the best way to complete it from a list of possible options.

Sentence, Summary, Note, Table, Flow-chart completion
(Listening and Reading) You listen to a recording, or read a text, and fill in the missing information. Sometimes you complete the task by choosing words from a box rather than words in a Listening/Reading text. There is a limit to the number of words you can use, so pay careful attention to this when you are deciding what your answer should be.

Form completion *(Listening)* You listen to a recording and fill in the missing information in a form. You must pay careful attention to the maximum number of words you can write for each answer.

Diagram label completion *(Reading)* You complete labels on a diagram which relate to a description contained in the text. You must pay careful attention to the maximum number of words you can write for each answer.

Short-answer questions *(Listening and Reading)* You listen to a recording, or read a text, and write short answers to questions. You must pay careful attention to the maximum number of words you can write for each answer.

Matching *(Listening)* You listen to a recording and match each numbered item to one of a list of options (A, B, C etc.) according to the information you hear.

Plan, Map, Diagram labelling *(Listening)* You listen to a recording and label the plan, map or diagram according to the information you hear.

How to revise for IELTS

It is important to use the time you have to revise for IELTS effectively. Here are some general ideas to help you do this.

Make a plan

It is a good idea to make a plan for your last month's study before the test. Think about:

- what you need to do
- how much time you have
- how you can fit what you need to do into that time.

Try to be realistic when you make your plan. If you plan to do too much, then you may soon be disappointed when you fall behind.

Think about what you need to know

Most things that you do in English will help you to improve your language skills – reading an article or watching certain TV programmes may be as useful as doing a grammar exercise.

It is very important, however, that you know exactly what you will have to do in the test. Doing some practice tests will help you develop good exam techniques and this will help you a great deal in the exam room. But don't spend all your revision time doing practice papers.

Think about which skills you need to improve. If you are attending an IELTS preparation course, ask your English teacher what you need to work on – listening, reading, writing, or speaking.

Look back at your homework. What mistakes did you make? Do you understand where you went wrong? How can you improve?

Have what you need to hand

In order to prepare for IELTS you probably need:

- a good learners' dictionary (one with examples of how words are actually used in English)
- some practice tests
- an IELTS preparation coursebook
- a good grammar book
- a vocabulary notebook
- notes or other materials from your English course (if you are doing one)
- a bilingual dictionary.

If you have access to the internet you can get some of these online – the dictionaries and samples of IELTS test materials, for instance. (See www.ielts.org and www.CambridgeESOL.org)

Also have a good supply of stationery such as pens, pencils, highlighters and paper. Some students find it convenient to write things like vocabulary on cards, which they then carry with them and look at when they have a spare moment on the bus or in a café.

Think about when and where you study

Most people find it best to study at regular times at a desk with a good light and everything they need beside them.

Some people find they work best in the early mornings, while others prefer the evenings. If possible, do most of your revision at the time of day which is best for you.

However, you may also find that there are other good times and places for you to study. Perhaps you could listen to some English on an mp3 player while you are doing other things. Or you could read something on your way to work or college.

Organise your revision time well

Allow time for breaks when you are revising – many students like to study for an hour and a half, for example, and then have a break for half an hour.

Vary what you do – sometimes focus on listening, sometimes on vocabulary, sometimes on writing. This will make sure that you don't neglect any aspect of the language and will also make your study more interesting.

It is sensible to do something completely different before you go to bed – go for a walk, read a relaxing book or watch a favourite film.

Enjoy your study

Find some enjoyable activities that help your English – listening to songs in English or watching a TV programme or DVD will generally help your listening and pronunciation and may also extend your vocabulary.

What do you like doing in your free time? Could you combine that with English practice? For example, if you like a particular sport or singer, or if you are interested in news or computer games, you will be able to find something in English about your interest on the internet.

Study with a friend – you can practise talking to each other in English and can perhaps help each other with any questions you have.

Keep fit

Don't forget that feeling fit and healthy will help you get good marks too:

- make sure you get enough sleep
- remember to eat well
- take some exercise.

Now here are some ideas to help you organise your revision for the individual parts of IELTS.

The IELTS Listening test

Even if you are a long way from an English-speaking country, there are a lot of things you can do these days to give you practice in the kinds of listening you will have to deal with in the IELTS Listening test. Here are some ideas:

- Go to the websites of universities in English-speaking countries – these often have links where you can listen to students or staff talking about the experience of studying in their institution.
- You can find TV and radio programmes on topics relevant to IELTS on the websites of national public broadcasting organisations like the BBC (www.bbc.co.uk/iplayer), PBS (www.pbs.org) and the Australian Broadcasting Corporation (www.abc.net). You can access some of these wherever you are in the world, but some programmes are only available to people living in the country where the broadcaster is based.
- Find the tourist information website for a country that you would like to visit – such websites often now have video clips which provide useful listening materials.
- Many libraries and museums now also have websites with video materials which can provide useful listening practice.
- Search YouTube (www.youtube.com) for interesting recordings – use keywords like 'lecture' or 'tutorial', or 'study skills' or 'lab reports' and you should find plenty of clips to help you practise.

The IELTS Academic Reading test

The more you read before the test, the better you will do. Reading is also a very good way of improving your vocabulary and grammar and it will also help your own writing.

In the Academic Reading test you will mainly have to read the kind of factual or discursive texts that have an academic relevance. It is therefore sensible to revise by reading plenty of texts of this kind. Look for articles in quality newspapers, magazines and journals focusing on academic topics (e.g. science, humanities, economics, current affairs, sociology).

- Make sure you read from a wide range of sources including something from each of the text types listed above – you can easily find examples of all of these on the internet as well as in printed form.
- It's important to read for pleasure, so regularly read something that you enjoy – novels, sports reports or magazine quizzes may not feature in IELTS but reading them will also help you develop your knowledge of the language in an effective way.
- Keep a reading diary – write a couple of sentences in English about what you have read. This should also help you to learn some of the words and expressions you have read and will also help you with the IELTS Writing paper.
- Discuss what you have read with a friend – perhaps start a reading club to do this on a regular basis.
- Don't look up every word that you are not sure about when you read. Just look up anything that seems to be important for a general understanding of the text. When you have finished reading you can then, if you want, go back and check the meanings of less important vocabulary.

Examples of things you might like to read include:
- graded readers and magazines
- translations of books you have already read in your own language
- travel information about your own country or places you have been to
- newspaper articles
- music, film or book reviews.

Other good sources of appropriate reading material for the IELTS Academic Reading test include:
- textbooks
- encyclopedia entries for topics that interest you
- language-learning materials that focus on academic vocabulary.

The IELTS Academic Writing test

In the Academic Writing test you will have to describe and explain a graph or other visual material (Task 1) and write an essay giving your opinion on a topic (Task 2).

Practise writing answers to exam type tasks on a regular basis – if possible, ask a teacher or other good English speaker to correct your work. Pay attention to the comments they make and try to improve in the next piece of writing you do for them.

- Always think about the structure of what you are going to write – make a plan first.
- In your writing make a point of using new words and expressions that you have recently learned – if necessary use a good learner's dictionary for good examples of how words are used in practice.
- Practise checking your writing carefully so that it is as accurate as possible – look particularly for the kinds of mistakes that you know you often make (mistakes with verb agreement, prepositions or articles, for example).

The IELTS Speaking test

Make the effort to practise speaking in English whenever you can.

- Make sure that you know how to talk about your own work and study experiences and plans – become familiar with the relevant language by reading articles on the internet about, for example, your chosen profession and about university courses.
- Make sure that you know how to express your opinion on a range of general topics, giving examples and reasons to explain why you think as you do – become familiar with the relevant language by listening to radio or watching TV programmes in which people give their opinions.
- If there are students in your area whose first language is English, try to make contact with them – perhaps you could exchange conversation sessions with them – half an hour in English and half an hour in your first language.
- Try to make contact with English-speaking visitors to your area.
- Practise with friends by agreeing only to talk in English for half an

hour on a regular basis – choose a specific topic to discuss for that time.

- Join an English language club if there is one in your area.
- Make sure that you can do these things with ease in English – introduce yourself, agree or disagree, ask someone to repeat or explain, give arguments for and against, make hypotheses, talk about your own experiences, justify a point of view – as you will almost certainly need to do most of these in the Speaking test.

We hope these ideas will help you to make the most of your revision time. Above all, we hope that you enjoy your studies and wish you all the best for your exam.

The IELTS Listening test

What's in the Listening test?

Section 1 a conversation in an everyday social context between two people

Section 2 a monologue in an everyday social context

Section 3 a conversation in an educational or training context between two or more people

Section 4 a lecture or talk on a topic of general academic interest

☑ 1 mark for each correct answer

 Approximately **40 minutes**
(including 10 minutes to copy your answers onto the answer sheet)

Each section has 10 questions.

The following question types are used in the Listening test:

- multiple choice
- matching
- plan, map, diagram labelling
- note completion
- form completion

- table completion
- sentence completion
- short-answer questions
- summary completion
- flow-chart completion

Any of these question types may appear in any section. Not all question types will appear in an individual Listening test.

Listening: multiple choice

 TIP: Don't choose an option just because you hear a word from it. Think about the whole meaning of what is said.

Example
Here is a question from a task about a field trip.

> **What did the students see on their walk in the mountains?**
>
> **A** a group of unusual animals
>
> **B** some rare plants ✓
>
> **C** an interesting geological feature

TAPESCRIPT

TUTOR:	How did you enjoy the field trip to Scotland?
STUDENT:	Well, we had some fantastic walks. One day we walked along an amazing deserted beach. We must have walked for about fifteen miles and we saw a seal which was basking in the sunshine. It was there all by itself.
TUTOR:	How lucky! They're such beautiful animals and it's quite unusual to see them there.
STUDENT:	That's right. Another day we climbed the mountain behind the hut where we were staying. We were hoping to find some rare ferns that are supposed to grow there and nowhere else in Scotland. We'd just about given up hope when we found some at the bottom of a rocky slope. They have a number of very interesting features, for example …

Explanation: The correct answer is **B**, but the mention of an unusual animal (a seal, although only one) might lead you to believe that **A** is correct. Similarly, the phrase 'interesting features' might tempt you to the answer **C**. In other words, you need to understand the recording as a whole rather than jump to a conclusion simply because you hear words from one of the options.

Listening: multiple choice

 TIP: Sometimes in a multiple-choice question you have to complete a half sentence with one of the options. If you change the first half sentence into a question it often makes it easier to choose the right answer.

Example

Here is a question from a task about a lecture on a scientific experiment.

 The study was carried out in order to

A determine the health benefits of eating tomatoes

B investigate whether tomato tablets could protect against heart disease ✓

C establish the side-effects of a range of nutritional supplements

TAPESCRIPT

As we are all well aware, some nutritional supplements have some undesirable side-effects. The Robinson research that we're going to look at today seems to have determined quite conclusively that the tomato tablets under consideration have no significant side-effects at all. However, his main focus was on their health benefits. It's long been known that a diet rich in tomatoes seems to be very good for our hearts. However, until recently it has been impossible to preserve the health-giving, antioxidant properties of tomatoes in tablet form. Robinson wanted to find out whether these supplements would really have the same health benefits as a tomato-rich diet.

Explanation: In this case the question would be 'Why was the study carried out?' and **B** is the correct answer. **A** is incorrect because the speaker says that the health benefits of eating tomatoes have long been known – there was therefore no need for a further study into this. **C** is incorrect because it relates only to the side-effects of tomato tablets (and not a range of nutritional supplements) and also because the issue of side-effects was not the main focus of the study.

Listening: multiple choice

 TIP: You will hear some reference to all the options in the list, but some of them will not be an appropriate answer to the question.

Example

Here is a question from a task relating to a student's lab report.

Q **Which TWO sections of her work does the student need to improve?**

A conclusion ✓

B figures ✓

C procedure

D results

E aims

TAPESCRIPT

STUDENT: *How was my lab report this time? Do you think it was better than my last one?*

TUTOR: *Yes, it was much improved, particularly the clear way in which you described the procedure. I also felt you laid out the aims very clearly, which gave a good impression from the start. You could think a bit more in future about the conclusions section, though. That felt a bit hurried to me even though you'd actually made a first-class job of writing up the results.*

STUDENT: *What about the way I presented the figures? Was that OK?*

TUTOR: *Yes, I liked it. But don't forget that you need to label them all and then you can refer to them more easily when you're describing them in your text.*

Explanation: The tutor suggests that the student can improve the conclusion **A** and the figures **B**.

The tutor makes positive comments about procedure **C**, results **D** and aims **E**.

Listen to everything the speaker says before you choose the answer, in order to be sure that you are selecting the correct options.

Listening: multiple choice

 TIP: You may find it useful to cross out each option that you hear being eliminated.

Example

Here is a question from a task relating to a lecture on languages.

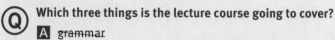 **Which three things is the lecture course going to cover?**

A ~~grammar~~

B language change ✓

C language families

D multilingualism ✓

E ~~pronunciation~~

F sociolinguistics ✓

G ~~vocabulary~~

TAPESCRIPT

Welcome to the first lecture in our course on linguistics. Today I'm going to start off with a brief look at the relationship between society and language and we'll continue with that topic next week. **— F** However, first I'm going to give you just a quick overview of what the course will cover over and above that first topic. So, last year we looked together at aspects of language such as vocabulary and how words combine to communicate meaning in a way that is considered 'grammatically correct' by the language's speakers. We're leaving these aspects of language now to take a slightly broader view. We'll look for instance at how people cope in societies where it's necessary for them to operate in more than one language. **— D** This is the case for a surprisingly large number of people who speak one language in their family and another at school or work. I'll leave for the moment issues relating to pronunciation as you'll be having a separate phonology course from Dr Thompson in the next semester. However, how languages have developed over time will be the third important theme of this course. **— B**

Explanation: The correct answers are **B**, **D** and **F**. Both grammar **A** and vocabulary **G** were dealt with last year. Pronunciation **E** will be covered on a different course. The speaker doesn't refer to language families **C** – he uses the word 'family' in relation to bilingualism.

The options don't follow the order in which you hear them on the recording. So make sure that you read them all first and keep them all in mind as you answer the questions.

Listening: matching

 TIP: The numbered items appear in the order in which you hear them, but the options (A–F) do not. Make sure that you read all the options before the recording starts.

Example
Here are two items from a task about finding temporary work.

 What does Jenny say about each type of job?

Jenny's opinion

A good opportunity to gain useful experience

B hours tend to be inconvenient

C jobs available for people with specific skills

D pay is surprisingly good

E plenty of work at the moment

F work is popular with students

Jobs

1 hotel work .....**D**....

2 telephone sales ....**F**....

 TAPESCRIPT

There are plenty of opportunities for temporary work in hotels available at the moment. It's quite hard work but you don't need any special skills. You can actually earn a lot more than you might imagine and it's often possible to choose the hours that are most convenient for you.

You might also be interested in doing something in telesales. It doesn't matter if you haven't got any previous experience of this. It's work which local undergraduates often choose to do. The hours tend to fit in well with lectures and other university commitments.

Explanation: 'You can earn a lot more than you might imagine' is another way of saying the 'pay is surprisingly good' **D**. The last two sentences make it clear, using quite different words, that the 'work is popular with students' **F**.

The words that you hear that give you the right answer may not be the same as the words on the page. On the other hand, you may hear the exact word from one of the options, but this does not necessarily mean that it is the right answer.

Listening: map labelling

 TIP: Listen carefully for the starting point – you need to start at the correct place in order to get the questions right.

Example
Here is the start of a task about a shopping mall.

Q Label the map below.

Waterside Shopping Mall

North entrance

Sporty Sports

A

West entrance

East entrance

Freshfields Supermarket

B

Brian's Music

C

Jones department store

South entrance

Toni's Shoes

Car park

You are here

1 pizza restaurant . . . . . .**B**. . . . .

TAPESCRIPT

OK, we're at the south entrance to the mall now. I'll tell you where some of the main shops are and then you can go off and explore on your own. Can we meet up though at the pizza restaurant at half past twelve? You'll find that about halfway along this street in front of us now. If you come to the fountain, that means you've gone too far. It's just before that on the left-hand side.

Explanation: It's very important to locate yourself in the right place. For example, if you start at the west rather than the south entrance then you will think the pizza restaurant is at **A** rather than **B**.

Listening: map labelling

 TIP: Use the pause before you listen to think about the words the speaker might use to describe the map or diagram.

Example

This example comes from a task relating to a motor show.

Q Label the map below.

- **A** biofuels exhibit
- **B** caravans
- **C** in-car entertainment
- **D** sandwich bar
- **E** sat nav developments
- **F** sports car stand
- **G** tyre technology

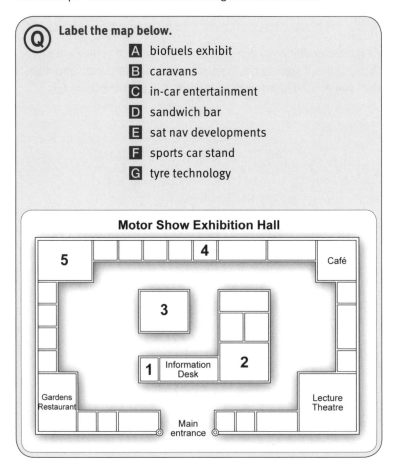

Motor Show Exhibition Hall

> **1** .... **C** .....
>
> **2** .... **A** .....
>
> **TAPESCRIPT**
>
> When you get to the Motor Show you'll find it's in an enormous hall and it would be quite easy to miss some of the most interesting exhibits, so I'd like to give you a bit of general information first. First of all, there is a small stand to the left of the information desk as you go into the hall. That's got a very interesting display looking at different modern technologies allowing you to listen to good quality music as you drive. Next to that, to the right of the information desk, is a very interesting area where you can see an area devoted to the development of more ecologically sound forms of petrol and diesel. I think that you will be impressed by what you see there.

C

A

Explanation: In this kind of activity you have to focus on what is in a specific place rather than on where something is. The numbers are on the map or diagram and you will hear them in the logical numerical order. It is unlikely though that the options will be referred to in exactly the same way as they are listed on the page. So you have to think in advance about how the recording might refer to the options. For example, if one of the options refers to 'biofuels' you might expect the speaker to use the words 'petrol' and 'diesel'. Similarly, when thinking about how 'in-car entertainment' could be paraphrased, you might predict the word 'music'.

Listening: matching

 TIP: Sometimes the **C** option is the **A** option plus the **B** option. Make sure that you wait to hear all the information you need before you decide on the correct answer.

Example

Here is a question from a task about facilities at a community centre and the first item from the list of facilities.

 When can the public use each of these facilities at the Community Centre?

      A Weekends

      B Monday to Friday

      C Weekends and Monday to Friday

Facilities

1 Swimming pool ...**C**...

 TAPESCRIPT

I'm pleased to say that this year Midtown Community Centre will be open to the public more than it was last year. The swimming pool has been extended and modernised and will be of great benefit to people of all ages in the town. As before, it will be open for schools every weekday during the day but everyone will be able to use it on Saturdays and Sundays from 7 in the morning until 9 at night. However, due to popular request it will now also be open for general use every evening during the week too.

Explanation: The first part of what the speaker says suggests that the answer is going to be **A**. However, it is important to continue listening, otherwise you will miss the information that public use is also possible from Monday to Friday in the evenings **C**.

Listening: note completion

 TIP: Listen for words that indicate the structure of the talk (words like 'first', 'next', 'finally' and so on) as these will help to guide you through the notes on the page.

Example

This is an example from a task based on a lecture about business organisations. You have to use no more than two words and/or a number.

 Complete the notes below.

Hofstede – study of **1** ... *cultural differences* ...

Analysed people in terms of:

- attitudes to change
- attitudes to **2** ... *power* ...
- masculine/feminine qualities
- individualist/**3** ... *communal* ... values

 Having looked last week at Weber's study of bureaucracy we're now going to go on and consider Hofstede's seminal work on cultural differences. He analysed 41 different nationalities and attempted to characterise them in terms of where they lay on four separate scales. Firstly, he considered how easy or difficult they found it to deal with change. Secondly, he looked at each nationality from the point of view of how they dealt with power. The next parameter related to the extent to which they exemplified what Hofstede refers to as masculine or feminine characteristics. And finally, he looked at whether the nationality's values tended to be communal or individualist.

Explanation: It is clear that **1** must relate to a topic for a study of some kind, **2** must relate to attitudes in society, and **3** must be an adjective that contrasts with 'individualist'. Preparing yourself like this before you listen will help you choose the right answers.

Listening: form completion

 TIP: Make sure that you are totally familiar with the names of the letters in English and the sounds which often cause you confusion. This task often asks you to write down words that are spelled out.

Example

Here is a question from a task about joining a social club. You have to write the name of the person who wants to join.

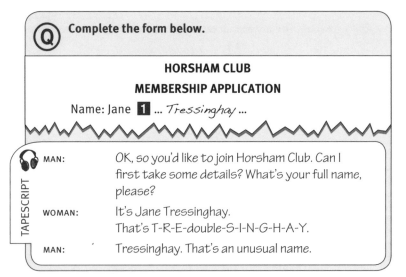

Complete the form below.

HORSHAM CLUB
MEMBERSHIP APPLICATION

Name: Jane **1** ... *Tressinghay* ...

TAPESCRIPT

MAN: OK, so you'd like to join Horsham Club. Can I first take some details? What's your full name, please?

WOMAN: It's Jane Tressinghay.
That's T-R-E-double-S-I-N-G-H-A-Y.

MAN: Tressinghay. That's an unusual name.

Explanation: Spelling questions are easy to get right if you know your alphabet in English. Practise with a friend if possible, so that it becomes easy for you. Practise dictating each other letters – and numbers too.

 *Reference numbers and postcodes often include both letters and numbers and these are often tested in form completion tasks.*

Listening: table completion

 TIP: Listen carefully – the recording may also include information that could fit in the gap but is not the correct answer.

Example

This example comes from a task about an arts festival. You have to use no more than two words and/or a number.

(Q) **Complete the table below.**

MARYBRIDGE ARTS FESTIVAL		
Event	**When?**	**Where?**
1 ... *poetry reading* ...	Friday, May 16th, 7 pm	**2** ... *Town Hall* ...

 TAPESCRIPT

This year's Marybridge Arts Festival will be hosting a large number of popular events and I'm here to tell you about some of them tonight. The Festival opens on Friday 16th May. There'll be an opening ceremony at 6 pm and that will be followed by a poetry reading. That will start at 7 pm and will feature a number of well-known performance poets. Please note that this event will take place in the Town Hall, but most of the other festival events will be in the Kings Theatre.

Explanation: Two events are mentioned in the recording – the opening ceremony and the poetry reading. The times of these make it clear that the answer to **1** is the poetry reading. Similarly, two venues are mentioned in the recording – the Town Hall and the Kings Theatre. You need to listen carefully to choose the right one for **2** (the Town Hall).

Listening: **sentence completion**

 TIP: Be careful that what you write fits grammatically with the other words in the sentence and is spelled correctly.

Example

This is part of a task in which two business students are discussing a group project. Use no more than two words and/or a number.

 Complete the sentences below.

1 This year's group project involves designing a ... *TV advert* ...

2 Meena missed the group project last year because of ... *computer problems* ...

TAPESCRIPT

TIM: I'm quite looking forward to this term's group project. I really enjoyed last year's one.

MEENA: Did you, Tim? I had to miss it, I'm afraid. You had to design a company logo, didn't you? Easier than planning a TV advert like we've got to do now.

TIM: You're right Meena. But why didn't you take part last year? Was it because of illness?

MEENA: Actually it was because I had computer problems and I just couldn't manage to sort them out in time!

Explanation: For **1**, if you just write 'advert' without 'TV', then it does not fit grammatically with the article 'a' and you would not get the mark. For **2**, if you just write either 'computer' or 'problems' it does not make total sense and you would not get the mark.

 *Remember to check your work carefully. Make sure that your grammar and spelling are correct.*

Listening: short-answer questions

 TIP: You will hear the exact word or words you need. You don't have to change them in any way.

Example

Here is a question from a task about booking a holiday. You have to use no more than three words and/or a number.

 Answer the questions below.

1 What does the man want to do on holiday?
... *see wild animals* ...

2 What kind of accommodation would he prefer?
... *self-catering* ...

 TAPESCRIPT

WOMAN:	OK, I can certainly make some suggestions for you about your trip to South Africa. But, first, I need to know what kind of thing you enjoy doing on holiday.
MAN:	Well, normally, my wife and I just like to relax on holiday, sunbathe, read, that sort of thing. But this is going to be a special holiday. So we want to see as much as possible, especially some wild animals.
WOMAN:	Well, there are lots of opportunities to do that there! So next, can you give me an idea about the sort of accommodation you'd like while you're over there? Luxury hotel? Guesthouse? Self-catering?
MAN:	Yes, that one. We do like to cook for ourselves.

Explanation: The correct answers are highlighted in the tapescript. There is no need to think of different words, for example, 'go on safari', to use in your answers.

Listening: short-answer questions

 TIP: Do not write more words than you are asked for – you will automatically lose marks.

Example

This is part of a task about plans for a study weekend. The instructions for this task tell you to write no more than two words.

 Answer the questions below.

1 What are the students going to study during the weekend? ... *romantic poets* ...

2 Which part of the weekend are they most looking forward to? ... *translation workshop* ...

TAPESCRIPT		
	MIKE:	It should be a good weekend, don't you think?
	FIONA:	Yes, I do. I love the romantic poets and to have a whole weekend studying them should be great.
	MIKE:	Well, it'll certainly be interesting to see how the English ones compare with other European ones, for example.
	FIONA:	Yes, I just hope the English versions of poems from other languages will be good enough to give us a real impression of what the originals were like.
	MIKE:	Well, the translation workshop should help us there. It focuses on how to translate poetry.
	FIONA:	Mm, I'm really looking forward to that most of all.
	MIKE:	Me too.

Explanation: You are asked to write no more than two words. If you write 'European romantic poets', 'the romantic poets' or 'the poetry translation workshop' you will not get the marks because you have written too many words.

Listening: summary completion

 TIP: Make sure your answers fit grammatically as well as reflecting the meaning of what you hear.

Example

This example comes from a task on the topic of product design. You should use one word only or a number in each space.

 Complete the summary below.

The QFD approach to product design is different from the so-called **1** ... *traditional* ... model in that it puts the requirements of the **2** ... *customer* ... first.

 Most engineers now prefer to take the QFD or quality function deployment approach to product design. This model has some significant differences in comparison with what is often referred to as the traditional approach. Of course it has to go through the same basic phases of establishing requirements, planning designs, producing and testing them. The focus, however, is that the customer and his or her needs are paramount and much more time is spent determining what exactly these are before work begins on any of the other phases.

Explanation: If you read the phrase containing the gap carefully before you listen, it will be clear that **1** needs an adjective or another word that could be used to describe a model or approach to product design. 'The' makes it clear that **2** will be a noun.

 *It's helpful to read the whole summary first before the recording starts.*

Listening: flow-chart completion

 TIP: You may think that you can guess the answer from your own world knowledge, but it is what the speaker says that is important and this can be different from what you might expect.

Example

Here is an example from a task about applying for a job. You have to use no more than two words and/or a letter in each space.

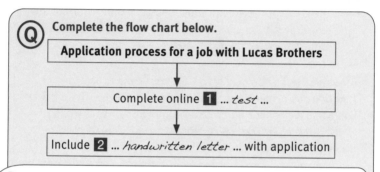

Q Complete the flow chart below.

Application process for a job with Lucas Brothers

↓

Complete online **1** ... *test* ...

↓

Include **2** ... *handwritten letter* ... with application

TAPESCRIPT

Now, I'd like to explain what the process is for those of you who would like to apply – or know someone who'd like to apply – for a position in one of our new offices. Of course we ask you to fill in an application form, but before doing that we'd recommend looking at our website where you'll find full details of what exactly we're looking for. That should help you to focus your application in the most appropriate way. On the site you'll also find a test which you can try to see how your profile matches what we're looking for. We ask you to do this first and there's space on our application form where you can fill in your scores. We don't require a photo or references at this point but we do also ask you to send us a handwritten letter with your application as we have also found that invaluable in our selection of new members of staff...

Explanation: From your knowledge of the world you might imagine that completing an application form is the first stage in the process of a job application, and the beginning of the recording might seem to confirm this. However, listening further it becomes clear that the answer to **1** is actually 'test'. Similarly, for **2** you might predict 'photograph' or 'references' but the correct answer is the less predictable 'handwritten letter'.

General tips for **Listening**

1 You only hear the recordings once – so write the answers as you listen.

2 Listen carefully to the introduction for each section and try to imagine what the speakers will talk about. This will give you useful information about the situation and the speakers.

3 In the real test, you have time at the beginning of each section to look at the task. Use this time well to read the questions and think about the topics.

4 The questions always follow the order of the recording. Don't panic if you miss one question – look ahead and think about the next one.

5 Write clearly when you transfer your answers to the answer sheet.

6 When you transfer your answers to the answer sheet, don't copy any extra words from the question paper.

7 When you read the question, you may find it helpful to think of words to listen for which have a similar meaning.

8 Listen to the intonation of the speaker as this could help you to decide whether the sentence is positive or negative.

9 It is useful to underline key words in the question to help you focus on the words (or similar words) to listen for.

 NOW YOU TRY! You will find a complete Listening test to try on the CD-ROM.

When you have finished you can see your scores, check and print your answers.

The IELTS Reading test

What's in the Academic Reading test?

 Three reading texts (with a total of 2,200 to 2,750 words) and 40 questions.

- texts come from magazines, journals, books and newspapers and have been written for a non-specialist audience
- at least one text contains detailed logical argument
- texts may include diagrams, graphs or illustrations

 1 mark for each correct answer

 60 minutes
(including time to copy your answers onto the answer sheet)

The following question types are used in the Academic Reading test:

- multiple choice
- identifying information
- identifying writer's views/claims
- matching information
- matching headings
- matching features
- matching sentence endings
- sentence completion
- summary completion
- note completion
- table completion
- flow-chart completion
- diagram label completion
- short-answer questions

Any of these question types may appear in any section. Not all question types will appear in an individual Academic Reading test.

Reading: multiple choice

 TIP: Use the key words in the question to help you find the right part of the text. Read the whole of that part, and consider all four options.

Example

Here is part of a text about poetry and one of the questions.

> Poetry is notoriously difficult to define. It is often regarded as the most personal of literary forms, in which the poet pours out his or her soul in an effusion of feeling. Yet there are numerous examples of impassioned prose, both fiction and polemic. Until a century ago, most poetry – in English, at least – used rhythm and rhyme, and the listener – for poetry is usually intended to be heard – could instantly recognise it as poetry rather than prose. Twentieth century developments have put paid to the utility of this distinction when characterising poetry as a whole, and, incidentally, given several generations the mistaken belief that poetry is necessarily hard to understand. The <u>defining characteristic of poetry</u>, surely, is that it evokes and heightens joy, sorrow, fear or myriad other emotions, and provides catharsis, the release of emotional tension.

 In the writer's opinion, the **main difference** between **poetry** and **other literature** lies in:

A the amount of effort it requires from the reader

B its use of rhythm and rhyme

C its effect on the reader ✓

D the extent to which it reflects the writer's feelings.

Explanation: The underlined and highlighted parts of the text show that **C** is correct because this is the writer's opinion. Remember the question as you read each option. **D** refers to the sentence beginning 'It is often regarded as', but this is not the writer's opinion. **A** is incorrect because it says this is a 'mistaken belief' and **B** is incorrect because it says that poetry no longer necessarily uses rhythm and rhyme.

Pay attention to phrases like 'in the writer's opinion' in the questions as the text may include several different points of view.

Reading: multiple choice

 TIP: Read to the end of the relevant part of the text, because the options are not in the same order as they are in the text.

Example

Here is part of a text about tourism and one of the questions. You have to choose two answers from the list of options (A–E) for this type of task.

> Mass tourism was made possible by the introduction of cheap flights and a boom in hotel construction. Both had a major impact on the environment, with construction particularly affecting Europe's Mediterranean coast. Mass tourism was primarily motivated by the wish of many northern Europeans to escape stress by spending time on beaches or beside a hotel pool in virtually guaranteed sunshine – which meant travelling to a more southerly country, such as Spain or Greece. This market was dominated by families and groups of friends, such as parties of young men holidaying together before the wedding of one of them.
>
> While such 'sun, sea and sand' destinations remain popular, a trend is apparent of giving greater importance to meeting individual needs rather than family needs. Holidays that include coaching by a golf professional or a cookery course, for instance, are attracting increasing numbers of participants.

 Which TWO of the following reasons for going on holiday does the writer mention?

A a wish to learn about other cultures

B an interest in developing skills ✓

C concern about the environment

D an intention to visit friends and relations

E a desire to relax ✓

Explanation: The highlighted parts of the text show you where you can find the answers. Remember that the information you are looking for is not always in the same part of the text. Here, you need to read to the end of both paragraphs to find the information which gives you the answers **B** and **E**.

Reading: identifying information

 TIP: Remember that the statements will not be expressed in exactly the same way as in the text, so look for key words in the statements and find similar words or phrases in the text.

Example

Here is part of a text about the history of Greenland and some of the questions.

> The <u>ancestors</u> of the Inuit people of Greenland are thought to have lived in <u>Siberia</u> – the vast eastern region of modern Russia – <u>until 7,000 or 8,000 years ago. There is evidence that they then <u>travelled</u> by boat into Alaska,</u> settling in the northerly part of <u>North America</u>. From there, some migrated to Greenland around <u>5,000</u> years ago, and <u>evidence has been found of their existence around the <u>northern tip of the island</u></u>.

1
2
3

(Q) **Do the following statements agree with the information given in the passage?**

1 The Inuit people are probably <u>descended</u> from inhabitants of <u>Siberia</u>. *TRUE*

2 The Inuit people's ancestors <u>migrated</u> to <u>North America</u> about <u>5,000</u> years ago. *FALSE*

3 The <u>north of Greenland</u> was the <u>most attractive</u> area of the island for the earliest settlers. *NOT GIVEN*

Explanation: The key words in the questions are underlined, and so are words in the text that they refer to. **1** has the same meaning as the first highlighted section. **2** The text says that they are thought to have lived in Siberia until 7,000 or 8,000 years ago. 5,000 years ago is when some moved from North America to Greenland. **3** No reason is given for migrating to northern Greenland. There is nothing in the text that 'most attractive' refers to, so the statement may or may not be true.

Reading: identifying writer's views/claims

 TIP: Remember that 'No' means the statement contradicts the writer's opinion, so it *can't* be right. 'Not given' means that there is no information about the writer's opinion in the text, so the statement *may* or *may not* be true.

Example

Here is part of a text about an art installation (or sculpture).

> At first glance, Cornelia Parker's 1991 installation *Cold Dark Matter: An Exploded View* would seem to be the outcome of a destructive drive in the artist's personality. On the contrary, she is fascinated by the way that change, even change of a violent nature, is a new beginning, an opportunity for something very different to emerge. *Cold Dark Matter* consists of a garden shed which Parker filled with objects, then asked the army to blow up. She suspended the resulting fragments in a room and lit them with a single bulb, throwing sinister shadows on the walls. The title is central to understanding the work, alluding to the cold dark matter which, in one version of the 'big bang' theory, led to the creation of the universe.

(Q) **Do the following statements agree with the views of the writer?**

1 The impulse for the work is the artist's psychological need to destroy. *NO*

2 The way in which the shed was destroyed adds to the meaning of the work. *NOT GIVEN*

Explanation: The highlighted parts of the text show you where you can find the information which gives you the answers. **1** can't be the writer's view because it contradicts ('On the contrary'). **2** Although there is information about how the shed was destroyed, there is no information about how this adds to the meaning of the work, so Statement 2 may or may not be true.

Reading: matching headings

 TIP: More than one heading may seem to match a paragraph at first. After reading the paragraph, read each heading and decide which one best sums up the main point of the paragraph.

Example

Here is part of a text about the scientific system for naming species of animals and plants. You have to choose the correct heading for each paragraph.

List of headings

i   Examples of the system in use

ii   Reactions to Linnaeus's work

iii   The origin of the system

iv   Which animals are lions and tigers related to?

A The scientific conventions for naming living organisms were established by the 18th century Swedish botanist, physician and zoologist, Carl Linnaeus, who developed binomial nomenclature, a two-word system for naming every species of animal and plant. The first word identifies the genus, and the second word is the specific name.

B As an illustration, lions belong to the genus *Panthera*, and their specific name is *leo*. Hence the species is classified as *Panthera leo*. Their relation the tiger, on the other hand, is named *Panthera tigris*. The two-word names indicate the relationship in a way that *lion* and *tiger* do not.

Explanation: Paragraph **A** explains how the system began, so the correct heading for **A** is Heading **iii**. Although the paragraph refers to Linnaeus's work, it isn't about *reactions* to it, so Heading **ii** is wrong.

In Paragraph **B**, two examples of animal names are given, using the system, so the correct answer is Heading **i**. Although the paragraph refers to lions and tigers, it doesn't refer to animals they are related to, so Heading **iv** is wrong.

You should read the headings before reading the text to focus your mind on the main ideas you need to look for.

Reading: matching features

 TIP: In the text, underline the names, dates, numbers, etc. from the questions or options, so that you can then locate them quickly.

Example

Here is part of a text about the development of fertilisers in the nineteenth century. In this example the questions follow the order of the text.

Food production was greatly improved in the nineteenth century, one reason being the development of effective fertilisers. The German chemist Justus von Liebig (1803–1873) added considerably to knowledge of plant nutrition, identifying the crucial importance of nitrogen, and the French scientist Jean Baptiste Boussingault (1802–1887) discovered that different kinds of fertilisers required different amounts of nitrogen. However, a business venture by von Liebig failed: although the fertiliser he sold was much less expensive than the guano it was intended to replace, crops were unable to absorb it adequately. Von Liebig later developed a manufacturing process for making beef extract cubes, which are still used in kitchens around the world.

In Britain, John Bennet Lawes (1814–1900) owned a farm where he experimented with crops and manures: at first he tested the effects of various manures on potted plants, and later worked on crops in the field. In 1842 he patented a successful superphosphate, which was the first artificial manure. Lawes made provision for the experimental farm to continue after his death, and it exists to this day.

1 He showed that nitrogen is essential for plant nutrition. **C**

2 He demonstrated the need to vary the quantity of nitrogen in fertilisers. **A**

3 He introduced a fertiliser that saved money but was ineffective. **C**

4 He invented a method of processing a food for human consumption. **C**

5 He invented the first synthetic manure. **B**

6 He set up a research establishment that is still in operation. **B**

List of Scientists

A Boussingault

B Lawes

C von Liebig

Explanation: The highlighted parts of the text show you where you can find the answers to each question.

Names and dates may appear more than once, so make sure you read all the relevant parts of the text.

Reading: **summary completion**

 TIP: Don't always expect words or phrases in the box to be the same as in the text. They may be words with similar meaning or the same word in a different form, so read both the text and the summary carefully.

Example

Here is part of a text about innovation in business.

Success, for many companies, depends on their ability to innovate, to create new products and services. Ask anyone which business sectors are the most creative, and the music industry will come fairly high up the list, but creativity is also the lifeblood of other, less obvious fields: the pharmaceutical industry, for instance, relies almost entirely on ideas and inventions that can be developed into new drugs. Just like land, buildings or machinery, ideas can be a valuable asset to a business, but while the former are tangible assets, with a physical existence, ideas are intangible, with no physical manifestation. Once an idea has been developed, whether into a new medical treatment or a new brand of clothing, it becomes intellectual property, and can be legally owned. It is then protected against competitors benefiting by imitating the new product without having had to fund its development.

Complete the summary using the words in the box below.

Innovation is **1** ... **F** ... for businesses in many sectors, from the most obviously **2** ... **D** ... , such as the music industry, to ones that are less self-evidently so, like the pharmaceutical industry. Like **3** ... **H** ... assets, new ideas may be very valuable, and so, like those, they need to be treated as **4** ... **B** ... to the business. They therefore require legal **5** ... **G** ... to prevent competitors from benefiting from the company's **6** ... **I** ... .

A intellectual	**B** belonging	**C** developing
D creative	**E** intangible	**F** essential
G protection	**H** tangible	**I** investment

Explanation: The highlighted words in the text show you where you can find the words which match the options. **1** 'is essential for' means the same as 'depends on'. **4** 'belonging to the business' means the same as 'property'. **6** 'investment' refers to 'to fund'.

Reading: note completion

 TIP: Only write the missing words, and make sure you don't repeat words from either side of the gap.

Example

Here is part of a text about the invention of cellophane. In this example answers should be no more than one word and/or a number.

> Cellophane was invented by Jacques Edwin Brandenberger, a Swiss chemist. In 1900 he made a coating to be applied to cloth, to protect it from being stained. The cloth was too stiff, but when he saw that the coating easily peeled off it as a transparent film, he realised the coating could be of value as a material in its own right. He eventually perfected the material, mainly by adding glycerine to soften it, and constructed a machine to make it.

 Complete the notes below.

Initial experiment:

- aim: to **1** ... *protect cloth* ... cloth from stains ✗
- problem: the cloth became **2** ... *stiff* ...✓
- potential value: the coating of film was **3** ... *transparent* ... and could easily be separated from the cloth ✓

Development:

- used **4** ... *glycerine to* ... to change the texture of the film ✗

Explanation: **1** is wrong, because 'cloth' is repeated. The correct answer is 'protect'. **4** is wrong, because 'to' is repeated. The correct answer is 'glycerine'.

Reading: sentence completion

 TIP: Make sure you use words from the text exactly as they are written in the text, and that they fit the sentences grammatically.

Example

Here is part of a text about public relations. In this example, answers should be no more than one word and/or a number.

> Not so long ago, public relations – or PR, as it is usually referred to – was the poor relation of many functions within an organisation. While Production, Finance and even Human Resources were usually represented at Board level, the PR function was much further down the hierarchy, simply expected to do its job of issuing press releases and gaining positive publicity for the organisation. This is now changing. In addition to these bread-and-butter tasks, PR specialists may now be involved in strategic planning, as senior managers realise how much PR can contribute as the ears and eyes of the organisation.

 Complete the sentences below.

1 Some of an organisation's other ... *function* ... used to be considered more important than PR. ✗

2 In the past, an organisation's ... *Board* ... was unlikely to include anyone from PR. ✓

3 The role of PR includes trying to ensure that the organisation attracts favourable ... *positive publicity* ... . ✗

4 PR now sometimes helps to develop an organisation's ... *planning* ... . ✓

Explanation: Although 'function' and 'functions' both appear in the text, in **1** 'function' is wrong because it would make the sentence ungrammatical. The correct answer is 'functions'. In **3**, 'positive publicity' is wrong because it would make the sentence ungrammatical, and 'positive' means the same as 'favourable'. The correct answer is 'publicity'.

Reading: table completion

 TIP: Use the information in the table to help you predict the type of word you need to find in the text. The answers may not follow the order of the text, but are generally in the same part of the text.

Example

Here is part of a text about a company called Sharp Corporation. In this example, answers should be no more than two words and/or a number.

One of Japan's major companies is Sharp Corporation, started by 18-year-old Tokuji Hayakawa in 1912, in Tokyo. At first the company worked with metal, producing snap buckles for belts, then, from 1915, the 'Ever-Sharp Pencil' – a mechanical pencil that gave the company its present name. The Sharp Group is now a major manufacturer of electronic goods, from LCD TVs to solar cells. It has expanded into 25 countries or regions around the world, and has a total of 60,200 employees worldwide, including 32,200 in its home country, where its head office has now moved to Osaka. The company entered the USA market in 1962, setting up Sharp Electronics Corporation (SEC), with its headquarters in New Jersey. SEC now employs 2,500 people.

 Complete the table below.

Company name	Date founded	Original products	Location of head office	Number of employees
Sharp Corporation	**1** ... 1912 ...	**2** ... metal ... goods	**3** ... Osaka ..., Japan	**4** ... 32,200 ... in Japan
SEC	**5** ... 1962 ...	electronic goods	**6** ... New Jersey ..., USA	**7** ... 2,500 ...

Explanation: The highlighted words in the text show you where you can find the answers. It is helpful to read the headings carefully, then read each line of the table across, from left to right. For example, 1 and 5 must be dates, 2 must describe some kind of product, and so on.

Use words from the text without changing them or using more than the maximum number stated.

Reading: short-answer questions

 TIP: Make sure you copy the words correctly and you spell them as they are spelled in the text.

Example

Here is part of a text about a vessel that is used to explore the depths of the ocean. Each answer should be no more than two words and/or a number.

> A great deal of research into the depths of the ocean has been carried out using the submersible Alvin, a craft that can carry three people down to a depth of 4,500 metres. Constructed in 1964, it is operated by the Woods Hole Oceanographic Institution (WHOI) in the USA.
>
> Alvin is manufactured from syntactic foam, a material which is strong enough to withstand the enormous water pressure that the submersible encounters. It is equipped with lights, two robotic arms to manipulate instruments, and a basket for tools and for samples picked up from the ocean floor.

 Answer the questions below.

1 In which year was Alvin built? … (in) *1964* … ✓

2 What material is Alvin made of? … *syntactic faom* … ✗

3 What equipment on Alvin can operate instruments?
… *robotic arm* … ✗

4 What equipment on Alvin is used as a container?
… (a) *basket* … ✓

Explanation: In **2** one word, 'foam', has been copied wrongly, so the answer won't get a mark. In **3** one of the two words, 'arms', has been copied wrongly, so this answer will be marked wrong.

The questions and answers follow the order of the text.

Reading: flow-chart completion

 TIP: To work out the order in which activities happen, try to identify particular words in the text that show this.

Example

Here is part of a text about the process of producing sugar. In this example, answers should be no more than one word and/or a number.

Raw sugar comes from sugar cane. When the cane is harvested, it <u>first</u> goes to mills, usually in the same region, and raw sugar is extracted from it. This is <u>then</u> sent in bulk to refineries, which are often located in heavy sugar-consuming countries. There are several stages in the refining process, <u>starting with</u> affination, which includes the removal of various impurities by using a centrifuge. <u>Eventually</u> the recovery stage is reached, which leaves white sugar and a sweet by-product which is often used as cattle feed.

Q **Complete the flow chart below.**

Sugar cane sent to **1** ... *mills* ...

↓

Raw sugar shipped to **2** ... *refineries* ...

↓

3 ... *Impurities* ... in the sugar are removed

↓

4 ... *Recovery* ... stage: by-product may be eaten by **5** ... *cattle* ...

Explanation: The underlined words in the text show the order in which activities happen.

Reading: summary completion

 TIP: The summary may be based on a part of the text. If the summary has a title, use this to help you locate the area of the text in which the answers may be located.

Example

Here is part of a text about a research method called 'participant observation'. Answers should be no more than two words and/or a number.

Participant observation

Cultural anthropologists often adopt a research method known as 'participant observation' to become familiar with a community's customs and behaviour, and to gain understanding of them. Users of the method immerse themselves in the life and culture of the people they are studying, with whom they interact in the community's natural environment. Their involvement often extends over a considerable period – some researchers have lived in the community they are studying for a matter of years. They may use a variety of methods, including informal interviews, group discussions and the study of personal documents, as well as observation. Through their involvement in the life of the community they expect to gain the perspective of an insider on the customs and behaviour of the group, while at the same time taking the role of an objective observer.

 Complete the summary below.

'Participant observation' is a research method sometimes used by **1** ... *cultural anthropologists* ... and other researchers to study a community in its **2** ... *natural environment* ... .

The research may require a commitment lasting several **3** ... *years* ... . The researcher's goal is to acquire some

> **4** ... *understanding* ... of the community's customs and behaviour by viewing them from the community's own viewpoint as an **5** ... *insider* ... , while simultaneously remaining a detached **6** ... *observer* ... .

Explanation: The title appears at the start of this section of the text. It is therefore a good place to start looking for the missing words, which have been highlighted in the text for you.

The answers may not come in the same order as the information in the text.

General tips for Reading

1 Read the instructions for each task carefully, and make sure you follow them, especially instructions regarding the maximum number of words.

2 Make sure you give the text a quick read through so that you are familiar with the topic and how it is developed in the text, but don't worry if you don't understand every word.

3 You can write on the Question Paper, but you must copy your answers onto the answer sheet within the 60 minutes, so allow time to do that.

4 Remember that every question gives you one mark.

5 Don't spend too long on any one question. Move on to the next question and go back if you have time.

6 If a text contains specialist or technical terms then a simple glossary is provided below the text. It is important to read this too.

 NOW YOU TRY! You will find a complete Reading test to try on the CD-ROM.

When you have finished you can see your scores, check and print your answers.

The IELTS Writing test

What's in the Academic Writing test?

Task 1 You have to describe some information contained in a graph/table/chart/diagram and present the description in your own words. The information may be data, the stages of a process, how something works or you may have to describe an object or an event.

You have to write at least 150 words.

Task 2 You have to write a short essay in response to a topic which is presented as a point of view, an argument or a problem.

You have to write at least 250 words.

 Task 2 contributes twice as much as Task 1 to the Writing score.

 1 hour
(about 20 minutes for Task 1 and 40 minutes for Task 2)

Writing: Task 1

 TIP: Whether you have to describe a graph, table or chart, think carefully about what you need to include in your description. Don't describe every detail of the information. Choose the most important and interesting features to write about.

Example

Here is an example of a Task 1 question using a bar chart.

> (Q) **The bar chart below shows different methods of transport to work in 1999 and 2009.**
>
> Summarise the information by selecting and reporting the main features, and make comparisons where relevant.
>
>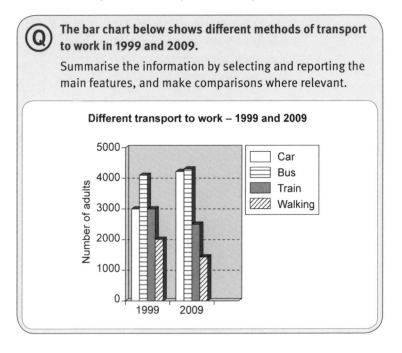

Here are some notes which a student made for this task.

Bus – the highest number of people using it / a
slight increase

Car – the second most popular / a large rise

Train – as popular as the car in 1999 / a fall

Walking – the least popular / a fall

Explanation: These notes are part of the plan for writing. They illustrate the most important features you could write about.

Writing: Task 1

 TIP: Support your description with figures, but you don't need to give every number exactly. You can be approximate by using words like 'over', 'about' and 'around'.

Example

Here is an example of a Task 1 question about overweight people.

 The graph below shows the percentage of overweight people in the population from 1993 to 2005.

Summarise the information by selecting and reporting the main features, and make comparisons where relevant.

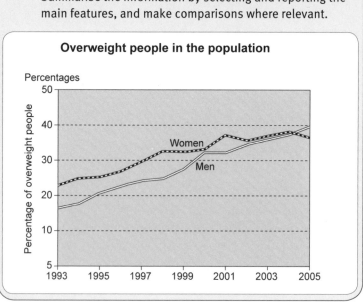

Here is part of what a student wrote for this task.

In 1993 about 5% more women were overweight than men, and over the whole period until 2004 women were more likely to be so than men. Between 2002 and 2004 the figures for men and women were very similar, with a slightly greater percentage of females being overweight during these years.
However, a higher number of men were overweight in 2005, with the percentage for women around 2% lower in this year.

Explanation: The highlighted words use approximate language to describe the figures and information.

Use language to compare things – 'more than', 'greater than', etc. This will help you to make comparisons of figures in charts, graphs and tables.

Writing: Task 1

 TIP: Sometimes you will have to describe a diagram showing a process. Identify all the stages of the process clearly before writing about it.

Example

Here is an example of a Task 1 question asking you to describe the process of making potato crisps from a diagram.

> **Q** **The diagram below shows the process of making potato crisps.**
>
> Summarise the information by selecting and reporting the main features, and make comparisons where relevant.

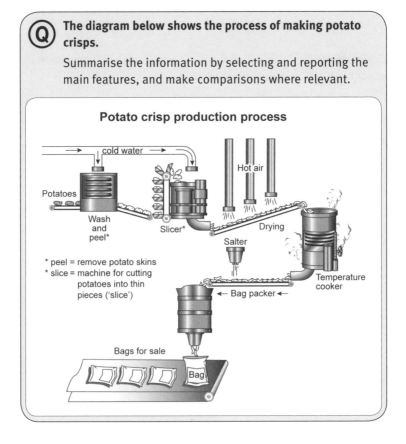

Potato crisp production process

* peel = remove potato skins
* slice = machine for cutting potatoes into thin pieces ('slice')

Explanation: Here are some notes made by a student before writing a summary identifying the seven stages.

1 *Potatoes are peeled and washed with cold water.*

2 *They are sliced.*

3 *They are dried using hot air.*

4 *They are cooked.*

5 *Salt is added.*

6 *They are packed in bags.*

7 *They are transported and sold.*

If there are any difficult technical words in the diagram, chart or graph, they will be explained.

Writing: Task 1

 TIP: Use words in your description that show the sequence of the process.

Example

Here are parts of a description by a student for the potato crisp production process from the task on the previous page. The highlighted words show the sequence of the process.

First of all, the potatoes are peeled and washed with cold water. After this they are carried by conveyor belt to be sliced and washed again. When they ...

Finally, the potato crisps are transferred into bags and transported to be sold in shops and supermarkets.

 TIP: Check your writing when you have finished. Use a checklist every time you practise writing.

Checklist	✓
Have you written at least 150 words?	
Have you included an overview of the information?	
Have you selected the most important information?	
Have you supported your points with examples?	
Have you compared things effectively?	
Have you used linking words to connect your points?	
Have you made any mistakes in grammar or spelling?	

Writing: Task 2

 TIP: Analyse the question. Think carefully about what you are being asked to do.

Example

Here is an example of a Task 2 question.

 Some people say that governments need to do more to prevent damage to the environment.

To what extent do you agree or disagree with this statement?

Here is part of a student's answer to this question.

I think it is very important for us to protect the environnement.

It is now possible for recyle the materiels which we throw away, so we must take more responsibility for this.

Our planete has not so many ressources so we must also use not so much oil and electricity and gas and water. And I think we should take care for pollution so that the future generations can breath the clean air.

Explanation: This question specifically asks for your view on whether governments need to do more to protect the environment. It does not ask you to write about environmental damage and its causes, or about what individuals need to do.

Writing: Task 2

 TIP: Decide on your position and then plan your writing carefully by making notes and organising them into paragraphs. Make sure that each paragraph has a clear focus.

Example

Here is an example of a Task 2 question.

 Some people say that governments need to do more to prevent damage to the environment.

To what extent do you agree or disagree with this statement?

Here are three different approaches to the answer.

1 Agree that governments need to do more and give reasons to explain your opinion.

2 Disagree that governments need to do more and give reasons to explain your opinion.

3 Discuss both positions and say that they are doing some things but there are more things they could do.

These notes by a student show how to write a plan for an essay structure for the first approach, agreeing with the statement.

Introduction

Great deal of damage done to the environment by industry, transport & other things. Terrible impact on the world. I agree governments must do more to stop this.

Para 1

Governments should impose pollution taxes on companies. Financial incentive to change behaviour.

Para 2

Strict penalties for causing pollution e.g. heavy fines.
Make those who cause damage pay to clean it
up.

Para 3

Governments should increase knowledge and education
about damage to the environment. More people will
take action to prevent harmful effects.

Conclusion

Previous points show why governments
need to do more. Climate change a result of damage.
Serious effects for everyone around the world.

Writing: Task 2

 TIP: Include examples to support your opinion.

Example

Here is an example of a Task 2 question.

 Some people say that governments need to do more to prevent damage to the environment.

To what extent do you agree or disagree with this statement?

Here is part of a student answer for this question, showing how you can use examples.

> If governments imposed heavy taxes on those companies that cause pollution to the environment, for example, a chemical factory polluting a local river or an airline using planes that cause high levels of carbon emissions, then there would be a serious financial incentive for them to change their behaviour and invest in cleaner, more environmentally friendly ways of conducting their businesses.
>
> Governments should increase knowledge and education about how damage is done to the environment. This could be through public information advertisements or funding television documentaries, for instance, which would reach a large number of people. The result of this would be that people would have more awareness of the causes of harmful environmental damage and would exert pressure on those responsible for it or boycott their goods and services.

Explanation: The highlighted parts of the text show how the student uses examples to expand and develop the points.

Writing: Task 2

 TIP: Leave enough time to edit and check your writing. It's important to look for grammar and spelling mistakes, which are easy to make when you are writing to a time limit.

Example

Here is an example of a Task 2 question.

 Some people say that governments need to do more to prevent damage to the environment.

To what extent do you agree or disagree with this statement?

Here is part of a student's answer.

These days a great deal of damage is being done to [environment]
the enviroment by industry, transport and other
businesses. This are having a terrible impact on the [is]
world and is a major factor in causing climate change,
which could be catastrophic for life on earth. [urgently]
Governments urgent need to do something to stop
this before is too late. [it is]

Explanation: The highlighted words in this student answer are examples of mistakes which you can easily correct if you check your writing. The correct versions for each mistake are shown in the boxes.

General tips for **Writing**

1   Make sure that what you write is relevant to the question.

2   Use a range of linking words to connect and sequence your ideas.

3   Use a range of vocabulary that demonstrates your knowledge of English.

4   In Task 1, make sure the information you write about reflects the chart/table/graph/diagram accurately.

5   In Task 2, make sure that you give your own view clearly and support it effectively.

6   Check your work. Do you have any particular mistakes that you often tend to make, e.g. leaving out articles? Know your own typical mistakes and check your work carefully for them.

 NOW YOU TRY! You will find a complete Writing test to try on the CD-ROM.

When you have finished you can compare your answers against the sample answers.

The IELTS Speaking test

What's in the Speaking test?

Part 1 ⓠ You answer general questions about yourself, your home/family, your job/studies, your interests and a range of familiar topic areas.

Part 2 ⓠ The examiner gives you a card which asks you to talk about a particular topic and which includes points that you can cover in your talk. You are given one minute to prepare: you can make some notes if you wish. You talk for up to 2 minutes, after which the examiner may then ask one or two questions on the same topic.

Part 3 ⓠ The examiner asks you further questions which are connected to the topic of Part 2. These questions give you an opportunity to discuss more abstract issues and ideas.

11–14 minutes
The whole Speaking test is recorded.

Speaking: Part 1

 TIP: Explain your answers by giving reasons for what you say.

Example

Here are some examples of answers to questions on familiar topics.

> **EXAMINER:** What's your favourite place to relax in your home?
>
> CANDIDATE: Oh, definitely the balcony because if it's warm weather I really enjoy sitting out there in the open air reading a book or just watching the world go by.

> **EXAMINER:** Have you ever cooked a meal for a lot of people?
>
> CANDIDATE: Yes, lots of times. I love cooking for other people. Recently I made a big dinner for some of my friends from college. Actually, it was all traditional food from my country and everyone said they really liked it.

> **EXAMINER:** Are you planning to see any films in the near future?
>
> CANDIDATE: Well, I've heard there's a new Will Smith film coming out so I'd really like to see that. I've seen most of his films already. In fact, I go to the cinema quite a lot.

Explanation: The highlighted words show how you can organise your responses and explain your answers.

Speaking: Part 1

 TIP: Be prepared to answer questions using different tenses and verb forms.

Example

Here are some questions and typical answers. These answers cover a range of time frames.

> EXAMINER: **How long have you had this job?**
>
> CANDIDATE: Well, I started working there about eight months ago and I'm hoping to continue with it until I go back to my country because I'm really enjoying the work I'm doing.

> EXAMINER: **Are you going to travel anywhere later this year?**
>
> CANDIDATE: Yes, I'm planning to visit Greece later in the summer with a couple of my friends. That's because we want to go and see the famous ancient ruins and relax on the beach for some of the time, of course.

Explanation: Look at the highlighted examples to see how a range of verb forms are used to talk about the past, present and future.

Speaking: Part 2

 TIP: Use the 1 minute preparation time to make notes about what you will say about all the points given.

Example

Here is an example of a Part 2 task. Use the points to make notes on the piece of paper which the examiner will give you in the test.

Describe a time you visited a friend's home for a special reason.

You should say:

- when you went
- who you visited
- what you did there

and explain why you visited your friend's home.

Here are some notes a student made in order to prepare for this task.

Lee's house – last Saturday evening
My best friend – met at school – often do things
together – go out, my place, his place
Prepared dinner – tidied up – had dinner – tea – music –
chatting
Normally see Lee at weekends – invited for dinner with
college friends

Explanation: Your notes will help you to organise what you say and remember what you want to talk about.

 *The notes are just ideas. You don't need to write full sentences. Find out the way to write notes that suits you best.*

Speaking: Part 2

 TIP: Give more details about each of the points you make.

Example

Here is part of a sample answer to the task on the previous page.

WHEN YOU WENT
I went to my friend Lee's house last Saturday evening. As he lives quite near me it only took me about ten minutes to get there and I stayed for several hours because he'd invited several of our other friends round for the evening.

WHO YOU VISITED
Well, Lee is really my best friend I'd say and I've known him for several years. We first met at school when we were about 16. He's a really great guy and we spend a lot of our free time together. We sometimes go out to different places together but also he often comes round to my place or I go to his.

WHAT YOU DID THERE
When I got there Lee was getting ready and he'd prepared a whole lot of food for everybody. Because he was busy with that I helped out by tidying up in the living room …

After dinner we all sat around drinking tea, listening to music and chatting about various things. Yes, I remember we were talking about the exam because several of us are taking it around the same time …

WHY YOU VISITED
Well, the main reason I went to Lee's house was that he'd organised a dinner for all of us, me and several of our classmates at college. I'd say it was really a social occasion – a chance to relax, eat together and just have fun chatting.

Explanation: Giving more details shows that you can enlarge on a topic and that you can use a range of vocabulary and expressions.

After you finish speaking, the examiner may ask you a question about the topic you've talked about. You only need to give a short answer to this question.

Speaking: Part 3

 TIP: Weigh up both sides of a question and give examples to support this. This will help you to tackle the more challenging questions in Part 3.

Example

Here is an example of the kind of question you might get in Part 3. It asks you to think more broadly about the topic of friendship and to discuss it in relation to wider issues.

> EXAMINER: **What kind of effect do you think changes in technology have had on the nature of friendship?**
>
> CANDIDATE: Well, of course mobile phone and computer technology, the internet and everything, have all had a big impact on the way we manage our relationships with other people. They can affect the nature of friendship in so many different ways. For example, on the positive side, if you're far away from your friends it's so much easier to keep in touch using the phone or the internet. On the other hand, a lot of people would say that personal relationships have suffered from excessive use of computers – people are less interested in what's going on around them and spend more time alone on the computer.

Explanation: The highlighted sections show the language which the candidate uses to cover both sides of the question and support the argument.

 *Relating abstract topics to examples helps you to deal with a question more clearly.*

Speaking: Part 3

 TIP: Give your opinion and develop your ideas by offering examples of what you mean.

Example

Here is an example of the kind of question you may get in Part 3 and part of a candidate answer.

EXAMINER: **What qualities do you think are important in a good friend?**

CANDIDATE: Well, as far as I'm concerned, some of the most important things are trust and being supportive. What I mean is that a good friend should be someone that you can always depend on and turn to if you need them and you would do the same for them. For example, if you lost your job, a good friend might help you out by lending you money. They would know that you would pay it back and that you'd do the same thing if they were in the same situation.

Explanation: The highlighted words show good examples of developing ideas by adding details and examples.

Here are some useful phrases for giving your opinion.

Giving your opinion

In my view ...

As far as I'm concerned ...

That's a difficult question ...

To be honest, I think ...

Generally speaking, I'd say ...

I'm not sure what I think about that ...

I have mixed views on that ...

Well, on the whole, I tend to agree that ...

My view is that ...

It seems to me that ...

If you ask me ...

Always give an opinion! It doesn't matter what your opinion is – you are being assessed on your language, not your ideas. The examiner wants to hear how wide your range of language is.

General tips for **Speaking**

1 Spend time before the test speaking and listening or reading in English rather than in your own language so you are 'thinking in English' when you go into the examination room.

2 Smile and relax – the more you smile the more relaxed you will feel. Don't let the fact that the test is recorded make you nervous – try and concentrate on what you are asked about.

3 Always speak clearly so that the examiner can hear you.

4 It's important not to sound flat, so use stress and intonation to make what you say sound interesting.

5 Don't speak too fast because it can be difficult to follow. Don't speak too slowly as you won't have the chance to say very much.

6 Use fillers like 'Well', 'So' and 'Let me think' to give yourself time to prepare what you will say without leaving a long pause.

7 Don't worry if you make a grammatical mistake – you are being assessed on various things, not just your grammar.

8 Try to use a wide range of grammar and vocabulary during the test. The examiner can only award you marks for the language you produce.

9 Don't worry if the examiner stops you before you have finished. The test is carefully timed and the timings for each part must be observed by the examiner.

 NOW YOU TRY! Watch the video of the Speaking test on the CD-ROM to see what an IELTS Speaking test is like. You can then print the Speaking test materials (examiner script and the prompt card for Part 2) and practise with a partner.

What to do on the day

Very few people like taking exams, but you can make the day of the exam easier if you make sure you know what to expect and what you will have to do before you go to the IELTS test centre.

Rules and regulations

For any exam you take, there are some rules and regulations about what you **must** do and what you **mustn't** do during the exam. Read through the rules and regulations below and if there is anything you don't understand, ask your teacher or the administrator at the Test Centre.

You must ...

- provide a proof of your identity (e.g. passport or national identity card) at registration and every examination session. Candidates taking the test outside their own country must produce a passport. This ID must contain a number, a signature, a date of birth and a photograph.
- provide two recent identical passport-sized photographs on registration.
- only have on your desk your identification, a pen/pencil and an eraser.
- switch off your mobile phone, pager or any other electronic devices and put them with your personal belongings outside the test room. (Any candidate who does not switch off their phone/ pager, or who keeps one in their possession, will be disqualified.)
- tell the test invigilator immediately if the conditions on the day of the test in any way impede your performance.

You must not ...

- impersonate another person or have another person impersonate you.
- attempt to cheat, copy the work of another candidate or disrupt the test.

- use or attempt to use, a dictionary, pager, spell-checker, electronic recorder or mobile phone for the duration of the test. Any candidate doing so will be disqualified.
- talk to or disturb other candidates once the examination has started.
- smoke, eat or drink in the examination room.
- use, or attempt to use, a dictionary.
- reproduce any part of the test in any format/medium. Any candidate doing so will have their test results disqualified and be liable to prosecution.
- remove any materials used during the examination. This includes, but is not limited to, examination papers, Speaking task cards, answer sheets and working paper.

Advice and information

We hope that all our candidates will have a positive experience of taking the IELTS exam. So, we have prepared some advice and information so that you know what to do if there are any problems on the day that you take your exam. Make sure that you have read and understood all the information and advice below before you go into the exam.

Make sure you attend on time

- Know the date, time and place of your examination and arrive before the scheduled start time.
- If you arrive late for any of the components, report to the supervisor or invigilator. You may not be allowed to take the examination.

Provide what you need

- Take into the examination room only the pens, pencils and erasers which you need for the examination.
- You must not use correction fluid or highlighters.
- Leave anything which you do not need, or which is not allowed, outside the examination room.
- You may not lend anything to, or borrow anything from, another candidate during the examination.
- Do not bring valuables as the test centre cannot be responsible for these.

Examination instructions

- Listen to the supervisor and do what you are asked to do.
- Tell the supervisor or invigilator at once:
  - if you think you have the wrong question paper
  - if the question paper is incomplete or illegible.
- Read carefully and follow the instructions printed on the question paper and on the answer sheet.
- Fill in the details required on the front of your question paper and on your answer sheet before the start of the examination.

Advice and assistance during the examination

- If you are not sure about what to do, raise your hand to attract attention. An invigilator will come to help you.
- You must not ask for, and will not be given, any explanation of the questions.
- If you do not feel well on the day of the examination or think that your work may be affected for any other reason, tell the supervisor or invigilator.

Leaving the examination room

- You may not leave the examination room without the permission of the supervisor or invigilator.
- You cannot leave your seat until all papers have been collected and you have been told you can leave.
- When you leave the examination room you must leave behind any paper used for rough work, clearly crossed through, and any other materials provided for the examination.
- Do not make any noise near the examination room.

Results

- Results are issued by test centres, usually 13 days after the test.
- Results may be delayed or withheld where any of the Rules and Regulations have been breached.
- In exceptional circumstances, results may be delayed and you may be required to retake one or more modules where the pattern of module results is highly unusual.

Answer sheets

The practice IELTS test on this CD-ROM is interactive and you type your answers on the screen. On the day you take the real IELTS test, you will receive paper tests, answer sheets (Listening and Reading) and a Writing answer booklet.

You can write on the question paper while you decide what the correct answer is. However, when you have made a decision, you **must** transfer your final answers onto the answer sheet which the supervisor will give you for the Listening and Reading tests. The answer sheet is double-sided – one side for Listening, the other side for Reading.

Ten minutes' extra time is allowed for transferring answers at the end of the Listening test. In the Reading test candidates are required to write their answers on the answer sheet during the time allowed for the test. **No extra time is allowed for transfer of the Reading answers.**

How to complete the Listening and Reading answer sheet
You can see an example of what the answer sheet looks like on the next pages. There are instructions on the answer sheets to tell you how you should fill it in, but here are the main things you need to know:

- It is very important that you use a pencil to write your answers on the answer sheet.
- If you have to write a word or phrase for your answer, please write clearly. If the markers can't read your writing, they won't know if your answer is correct or not.
- If you change your mind about an answer, it is important that you use an eraser to rub out the answer you don't want.

How to complete the Writing answer sheet
You can see an example of what the answer sheet looks like on the next pages.

- You can use pen or pencil for the Writing test.
- You must write clearly.

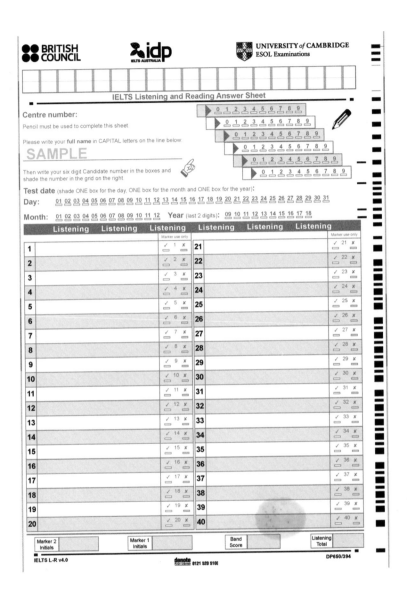

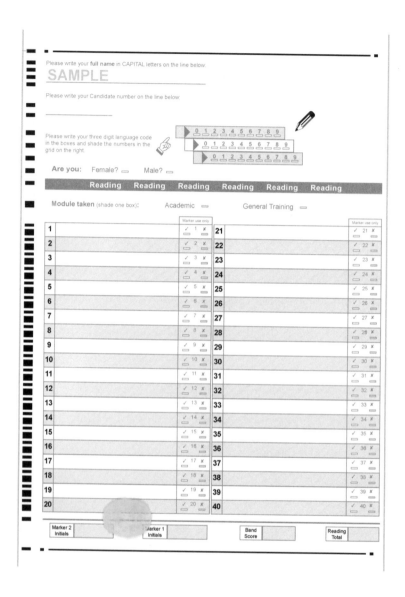

INTERNATIONAL ENGLISH LANGUAGE TESTING SYSTEM

 ●● BRITISH
●● COUNCIL

 IELTS
AUSTRALIA

 **UNIVERSITY** *of* **CAMBRIDGE**
ESOL Examinations

WRITING ANSWER BOOKLET

Candidate Name: ....   Candidate Number: ....

Centre Name: ....   Date: ....

Pretest Version Number: ....   First Language: ....

Module: ACADEMIC ☐   GENERAL TRAINING ☐   (Tick as appropriate)

TASK 1

_____

_____

_____

_____

_____

_____

_____

_____

_____

_____

_____

_____

_____

_____

| EXAMINER'S USE ONLY |

EXAMINER 2 NUMBER: ....

CANDIDATE NUMBER: ....   EXAMINER 1 NUMBER: ....

TASK 2

EXAMINER'S USE ONLY

_____

_____

_____

_____

_____

_____

_____

_____

_____

_____

_____

_____

_____

_____

_____

_____

_____

_____

_____

_____

_____

_____

EXAMINER'S USE ONLY			

EXAMINER 2
TASK 2

TR	CC	LR	GRA

UNDERLENGTH	NO OF WORDS	PENALTY
OFF-TOPIC	MEMORISED	ILLEGIBLE

EXAMINER 1
TASK 2

TR	CC	LR	GRA

UNDERLENGTH	NO OF WORDS	PENALTY
OFF-TOPIC	MEMORISED	ILLEGIBLE

Understanding your IELTS scores

Your performance in the real IELTS test will be reported in two ways: there will be a Band Score from 1 to 9 for each of the skills; and an Overall Band Score from 1 to 9. Both the Band Scores for each skill and the Overall Band Score may be reported in whole or half bands. The Overall Band Score is the average of your scores in the four skills. For example, if you score Band 6 for Listening, Band 6 for Reading, Band 5 for Writing and Band 7 for Speaking, your Overall Band Score will be:

$$\frac{6 + 6 + 5 + 7}{4} = \frac{24}{4} = 6$$

You will see from this example that a lower score in one skill can be compensated for by higher scores in the others.

Institutions or organisations considering your application are advised to look at both the Overall Band Score and the Band Scores for each skill to make sure that you have the language skills needed for a particular purpose. For example, if your course has a lot of reading and writing but no lectures, listening comprehension might not be very important and a score of, say, 5 in Listening might be acceptable if the Overall Band Score was 7. However, for a course where there are lots of lectures and spoken instructions, a score of 5 in Listening might be unacceptable even though the Overall Band Score was 7.

However, for the interactive Practice Test on this CD-ROM your scores will be reported differently. You will find out at the end of the test whether each of your answers was right or wrong and find out if your performance is likely to be acceptable.

The interactive Practice Test on the CD-ROM has been checked so that it is approximately the same level of difficulty as the real IELTS test. However, we cannot guarantee that your score in the *Top Tips* Practice Test will be reflected in the real IELTS test. The Practice Test can only give you an idea of your possible future performance and it is up to you to decide whether you are ready to take IELTS.

Installing the CD-ROM

Please set your screen resolution to 800 x 600 to get the best out of your *Top Tips for IELTS (Academic)* CD-ROM.

For Microsoft Windows

1. Insert the *Top Tips for IELTS (Academic)* CD-ROM into your CD-ROM drive. If you have Autorun enabled, Windows will automatically launch the Installation wizard for installing *Top Tips for IELTS (Academic)*. If not, double click the Top_Tips_for_ IELTS (A).exe from the CD-ROM.
2. Follow the Installation wizard steps.
3. After the installation completes, you can access the application from the Start menu.
4. You can also launch the application by double clicking the shortcut on the Desktop.
5. To uninstall the application, click Uninstall Top Tips for IELTS (Academic) from the Start menu.

For Mac OS X (10.4 or later)

Top Tips for IELTS (Academic) is distributed as a package ('.pkg') file for Mac OS X:

1. Insert the *Top Tips for IELTS (Academic)* CD-ROM into your CD-ROM drive. The *Top Tips for IELTS (Academic)* icon will appear on your Desktop.
2. Double click the icon. Mac OS X will display the contents of the CD-ROM.
3. Double click the file 'Top Tips for IELTS (Academic).pkg'. This will launch the Installer.
4. Simply click Continue on the Installer's Welcome screen to proceed with the installation.
5. Just before the Installer copies the files, you will need to enter the administrator's password.
6. After the installation is completed, the *Top Tips for IELTS (Academic)* application will reside as a folder named *Top Tips for IELTS (Academic)* inside the Applications folder.
7. Double click the *Top Tips for IELTS* folder to view its contents.

8. Then double click the *Top Tips for IELTS (Academic)* file to launch *Top Tips for IELTS (Academic)*.
9. NOTE: To easily open *Top Tips for IELTS (Academic)*, you can drag it to the dock.
10. To uninstall the application move the *Top Tips for IELTS (Academic)* folder from the Applications folder to the Trash.

System requirements

For PC

Essential:	Windows 2000, XP or Vista, CD drive and audio capabilities
Recommended:	400 MHz processor or faster, with 256mb of RAM or more

For Mac

Essential:	Mac OS X, version 10.4 or higher
Recommended:	400 MHz G3 processor or faster, with 256mb of RAM or more